Practical

SHOYU
COOKING

delicious dishes with Japanese soy sauce

by Chu Shinojima and Tamako Ashihara

JP

JAPAN PUBLICATIONS, INC.

Practical Shoyu Cooking

©1969 by Chu Shinojima and Tamako Ashihara

First Printing, 1969
Second Printing, September 1972

Library of Congress Catalog Card Number 68–58252
ISBN-0-87040-110-6

Published by
JAPAN PUBLICATIONS, INC., Tokyo

Distributed by
JAPAN PUBLICATIONS TRADING COMPANY
1255 Howard St., San Francisco, Calif. 94103, U.S.A.
P.O. Box 5030 Tokyo International, Tokyo, Japan

Photographs by Hisamitsu Yasumuro
Illustrations by Kazuko Terashima

Printed in Japan by Toppan Printing Co., Ltd.

INTRODUCTION

The Japanese Islands, on the far edge of the Pacific Ocean, stretch from the subtropics in the south to the near-arctic in the north. The four seasons of the year are clearly divided and each season brings its own special foods. Of course, the preparation differs with different seasons and dishes. And the foods fit their respective seasons as though some authority in ancient times had decreed this is the way it would be.

Certainly that is at least in part true for the history of Japanese cooking goes back over 1,000 years. During that time Chinese foods and dishes were introduced from the nearby mainland and, later, Dutch and Portuguese traders brought European cooking methods with them on their sailing ships. All of these were assimilated into traditional Japanese methods and entirely new ways were the result.

For example, at one time in our history Buddhist teachings forbid the eating of meat. Milk, butter, and other dairy products first came to be eaten only one hundred years ago. In this past hundred years increasing contact between Japan and the rest of the world has caused constantly increasing changes in traditional eating habits and cooking methods.

One important characteristic of Japanese cooking even today is that there is a constant attempt to put the basic ingredients to the best use in the simplest way. One means of accomplishing this is through the use of shoyu (Japanese soy sauce). Salt is almost never found on the dinner table in Japan but shoyu is always there. Shoyu has its own fragrant smell and effectively brings out the flavor of a wide variety of foods. Naturally, the use of shoyu is not limited to Japanese cooking alone and we hope you will come to enjoy it in all your cooking.

HELPFUL HINTS ON HOW TO USE THIS BOOK

In writing this book we have attempted to keep the use of ingredients and utensils restricted to those ones which can be found in most homes and/or markets abroad.

For the sake of simplicity we have avoided using Japanese words in this book. However, here are a few words which it will be useful for you to remember:

Miso: bean paste. Several types are available.

Mirin: Sweet rice wine chiefly used in cooking.

Sake: Japanese rice wine.

Suimono: clear Japanese traditional soup.

Shoyu: Japanese soy sauce. (See the section on shoyu also.)

Tofu: soybean curd. Comes in soft, whitish blocks.

The Japanese word for dried kelp is konbu or wakame. (These articles can be purchased in large food stores or in stores specializing in imported foodstuffs.)

You will find that Japanese cooks do a great deal of cutting and slicing. Meat is often cut completely away from the bone and vegetables are diced or sliced or cut into strips. This attention to delicacy is also carried over into the measuring of the ingredients themselves. The required amount of almost every item is exactly measured. However, do not let this discourage you from experiments and varying the ingredients to find the combination that pleases everyone best.

Minced ginger and minced leeks are often used as a garnish but naturally you do not have to if they do not suit your taste. You should try dried kelp if you can obtain it where you live but if not substitute an artificial seasoning in the recipes which call for kelp. Remember also that in Japanese cooking green vegetables are usually boiled very quickly so they do not lose their color or become too soft. As for the shoyu do not hesitate to vary the amounts called for to suit individual tastes. However, in the beginning it would be best to follow the recipe fairly closely.

One important point to keep in mind: these recipes are just like ones Japanese wives and mothers use and *rice is almost always served with these dishes.* In Japan the ingredients given in these recipes would be sufficient for a family of four. *So if you do not serve rice or if your family is larger or hearty eaters you should increase the amounts accordingly.*

You will find the approximate number of calories for each recipe above the ingredients. However, this figure represents the amount for each individual serving.

It is our sincere hope that you and your family find the dishes in this book as enjoyable to eat as Japanese families do.

Unit Comparison Chart

weight	g.	oz.	lb.
1 g.	1	0.035	0.002
1 oz.	28.35	1	0.063
1 lb.	453.5	16	1
length	cm.	in.	
1 cm.	1	0.394	
1 in.	2.54	1	

CONTENTS

Egg Dishes

Thick-fried Eggs
Fried Chicken and Eggs
Fried Eggs Wrapped around Chicken
Spinach Wrapped in Eggs
Egg Tofu
Two Color Eggs
Meat Wrapped in Eggs
Bamboo Wrapped Eggs
Special Scrambled Eggs

Thick-fried Eggs

There are some 40 ways to fry eggs in Japan but in this book we included only the ones which we felt you and your family would like best.

This dish is one of the most popular egg dishes. In Japan it is often used in lunch boxes and as a sweet egg dish for children.

INGREDIENTS (139 cal.)

    6 eggs
    4 tbs. water
    3 tbs. sugar
    ½ tsp. salt
    1 tsp. shoyu
    1 tbs. sake (not necessary if none is obtainable)
    1 tbs. salad oil for use in frying

PREPARATION

Break the eggs into a bowl. Mix them with a fork. (If a beater is used the texture of the eggs becomes too frothy and they are difficult to fry.) Mix in the water, sugar, salt, shoyu, and the sake (although this is optional).

Next, heat a frying pan and cover the bottom with the salad oil. When the salad oil has covered the bottom of the pan pour off any extra oil into a small dish. If there is too much oil it is difficult to fry the eggs properly. After the frying pan has heated turn the flame down low and pour in ⅓ of the egg mixture you have just prepared. As the mixture starts to fry spread it flat with a fork

Thick-fried Eggs

and when it is approximately half cooked fold it over on itself 3 times starting from the edge opposite you.

Pour the extra salad oil from the dish onto a paper towel and wipe the part of the bottom of the pan that now no longer has egg on it. Then move the egg omelet to that side of the pan and wipe the now empty part of the pan with the oily towel. Pour ½ of the remaining mixture into the available area of the pan while lifting part of the already fried eggs up to allow some of the mixture to run underneath. Again, when the mixture is half cooked fold the eggs over in the same way you did the first time. Now repeat the process once again. (see illustration) If any mixture remains it can be fried into shape with the use of a spatula.

If you wish a square shape wrap the cooked omelet firmly in a cloth and press both sides with something flat until it cools. After the shape is made cut the omelet into ½ inch thick pieces and serve.

Fried Chicken and Eggs

There are many dishes in Japanese cooking which call for both chicken and eggs. We also cook eggs with other kinds of fowl and with beef too. The dish below is so popular its one you'll find most anywhere in Japan. (See the section on Thick-fried Eggs before you cook this dish.)

INGREDIENTS (150 cal.)

> 7 oz. lb. chicken
> 3½ oz. mushrooms
> 3 tbs. shoyu
> 3 tbs. sugar
> 4 eggs
> oil

PREPARATION

Cut the meat into strips about ¾ of an inch. Cut the stems from the mushrooms, wash them, and slice into thin slices. Heat the chicken, mushrooms, shoyu, and the sugar in a pan. Break and mix the eggs and add them to the chicken and mushrooms. Heat a frying pan and put some oil in it. Pour ⅓ of the chicken and eggs into the pan and fry it. Fold it into threes. Fry the rest of the mixture the same way ⅓ at a time. Keep the shape long and narrow. Cut into individual portions and serve.

Fried Eggs Wrapped around Chicken

Eggs fried this way can be made hours before eating and the flavor will not change. Good for lunch boxes or situations where you have to prepare the food ahead of time. (See the section on Thick-fried Eggs before you cook this dish.)

INGREDIENTS (190 cal.)

> 10½ oz. chicken
> 4 eggs
> ¼ cup shoyu
> 1 tbs. or more sugar
> grated giant white Japanese radish
> small amt. shoyu
> small amt. oil

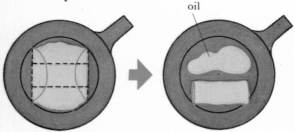

Fold over three times.

Add more egg mixture.

The eggs will look like this when fried.

12

PREPARATION

Slice the chicken meat into thin bite-size pieces. Mix the shoyu and the sugar and heat until ⅓ of the total amount evaporates.

Without using any oil or anything fry the chicken on a frying screen or frying pan. In order to keep the chicken from burning paint it about 3 times with a brush dipped in the shoyu-sugar sauce after it has fried a bit. If you paint the chicken before you start to fry it the surface will fry too quickly so remember to start with nothing on the chicken.

Now heat a frying pan and put some oil in it. Break and mix the eggs and fry them ⅓ at a time. When the first ⅓ has fried put the chicken meat on it and fold it over 3 times. Fry the remaining eggs the Thick-fried Eggs method. Cut into individual portions and serve. Each bite should be dipped into the grated white radish mixed with a little shoyu.

Spinach Wrapped in Eggs

This is a fried egg roll with spinach in the center. The contrast of the green and the yellow is quite attractive. It is not very sweet so it might be a more suitable dish for adults.

INGREDIENTS (107 cal.)

- 4 eggs
- 1 tbs. water
- 1 tbs. sugar
- ½ tsp. salt
- 1 tbs. sake (not essential)
- 1 tbs. salad oil for frying
- 4 bunches of spinach
- 2 tsp. shoyu
- 1 tbs. butter

PREPARATION

Boil the spinach in hot water to which a little salt has been added for one minute. After boiling for one minute soak the spinach in cold water to cool it. While maintaining the natural shape of the spinach press it firmly to remove the moisture. Then fry lightly in a tablespoon of butter.

Now break the eggs into a bowl and mix them. Add the water, sugar, salt, and the sake. (for mixing method see the recipe for Thick-fried Eggs)

Heat the frying pan and pour in the salad oil. Turn the flame down low and pour in ¼ of the egg mixture. When the eggs have hardened a little put all the spinach in arranged so that the stems of one bunch are on the leaves of the bunch below. Then roll the eggs over the spinach bunches starting with the side opposite you. (The eggs are to be fried and rolled the same way as in the recipe for Thick-fried Eggs. Please see that section.) Continue frying the remaining egg mixture in this way ¼ at a time until it has all been used. Once the roll shape becomes solid take the roll out and cut it into 1 inch lengths. Pour a little shoyu on and into the spinach at the end of each piece before serving.

Egg Tofu

This could be called a Japanese-style custard. There is no sweetness whatsoever. Chilled it can be eaten as a summer hors d'œuvre or in egg dishes. Hot it can be used in soups.

INGREDIENTS (117 cal.)

- 6 eggs
- 1½ cup soup broth
- ½ tsp. salt
- 1 tbs. sake
- artificial seasoning

PREPARATION

Break and mix the eggs. Add the soup broth (this can be made from simply water

Fried Eggs Wrapped around Chicken

Spinach Wrapped in Eggs

and artificial seasoning), salt, and the sake. In order to keep the mixture very thin pour it thru a fine strainer. Spread foil along the sides of a small box or empty can in such a manner that the foil can be removed later by its edges. Now pour the strained mixture in and remove any foam with a spoon.

Boil water in a steamer so that it steams and then turn the flame down low. Steam the box or can for from 15 to 20 minutes. If the flame is too high the texture will be thick so the secret is to steam slowly over a low flame.

This can also be down in a pan in an oven as long as there is water giving off some not too strong steam. If you can poke a toothpick or something similar into the mixture and clear watery liquid appears you'll know its done.

After it is done remove the foil. Here we have made a plum blossom shape but you can cut it into whatever shape or size you wish. It can be eaten as is when cold but the taste is a little weak so you might add shoyu or even mayonnaise. A little grated ginger or horse-radish mixed in will accent the taste.

Two Color Eggs

In Japan many special dishes are prepared for celebrating New Years and this is one of them. This dish could probably be used as a dessert.

INGREDIENTS (180 cal.)

    6 eggs
    6 tbs. sugar
    small amt. salt

PREPARATION

Boil the eggs and then separate the yolks from the whites. Grate or mash with a fork both the yolks and whites separately. If you do not grate the whites quickly while they are still warm they will harden and make it difficult. The yolks can be easily grated even after cooling.

The whites contain much moisture so wrap them in a cloth and squeeze it out. Add 3 tablespoons of sugar and a little salt to both the whites and the yolks. Spread wax paper in the bottom of a small box so that it can be removed easily later on. Put the whites in first; and after flattening them put the yolks

Egg Tofu

over as the second layer. Steam for from 7 to 8 minutes in a steamer. A double boiler can also be used for this. After they cool cut up as desired and serve.

Meat Wrapped in Eggs

This dish consists of ground meat wrapped in barely fried eggs. It is delicious either hot or cold.

INGREDIENTS (340 cal.)

    3 eggs
    2 tsp. cornstarch
    ¼ tsp. salt
    1 tbs. sake or water
    1 tbs. salad oil for frying

    9 oz. ground pork
    2 tbs. finely chopped onion
    1 tbs. finely chopped ginger root
    1 egg yolk
    ½ tsp. salt
    2 tsp. shoyu
    1 tsp. sugar
    1 tbs. cornstarch

    2 tbs. flour
    1 egg white

PREPARATION

Break the eggs into a bowl and mix. Next in another bowl mix the cornstarch with the sake (or water). Then mix the salt and the cornstarch paste in with the eggs. Pour the salad oil into a frying pan and when the bottom of the pan is covered pour off any excess. Turn the flame down low and pour half of the mixture into the pan spreading it out flat. When the upper surface has hardened flip the eggs over and fry for from 40 to 50 seconds taking care not to burn them. Now in the same way make one more "pancake" of eggs. (Using a Teflon pan will make this much easier.)

Two Color Eggs

Now put the ground pork into a bowl together with the finely chopped onion and ginger, egg yolk, salt, shoyu, sugar and the cornstarch. Knead until thoroughly and completely mixed. Next mix the egg white and the flour together a little at a time. It will turn into a thick paste. Spread this paste thinly over the lightly fried egg "pancakes." Spread half of the ground pork mixture out flat and onto one of the paste covered egg "pancakes." Roll it up from the edge using some of the paste to keep this egg and meat roll closed. Do the same for the other roll. Then take a wet cloth and tightly wrap the two rolls up separately. Put them both into a steamer and steam over a low flame for about 20 minutes. If the flame is too strong the eggs will unroll so be sure to steam slowly over a low flame. Wrapping in foil and baking in an oven on low heat for 20 minutes is an alternative method.

When done cut into half inch thick pieces and serve.

Bamboo Wrapped Eggs

When cooked this dish reminds us of narrow bamboo plants so we call it "Bamboo Wrapped Eggs." In cooking this dish we use both salt and pepper although pepper is not a common ingredient in Japanese cooking. However, pepper was introduced to Japan many centuries in the past. This is a delicious breakfast meal easy to prepare. (See the section on Thick-fried Eggs before you cook this dish.)

INGREDIENTS (210 cal.)

- 5¼ oz. pork
- small amt. salt
- small amt. pepper

- ⅓ onion
- 4 eggs
- ¼ tsp. salt
- small amt. pepper
- small amt. grated giant white Japanese radish
- small amt. shoyu
- small amt. oil

PREPARATION

Cut the pork into long narrow strips of about ½ in. Sprinkle a little salt and pepper over the strips and fry in oil.

Chop the onion up and fry in oil; then mix it in with the eggs together with ¼ teaspoon of salt and a little pepper for taste. Heat a frying pan and put some oil in. Fry ⅓ of the egg mixture. Put the pork in the center of the fried eggs and fold the eggs over twice. Fry the rest of the egg mixture the Thick-fried Eggs method. Keep the shape of the eggs the same as that of the first batch. Divide into individual portions and serve together with the grated white radish mixed with a little shoyu. Each bite should be dipped into this sauce.

Special Scrambled Eggs

This dish could be called Japanese-style scrambled eggs. Fried into the eggs are chicken and vegetables or anything you wish to add.

INGREDIENTS (223 cal.)

- 3 chicken fillets
- 1 3½ in. carrot
- 6 mushrooms
- 1 leek
- 2 tbs. green peas
- 2 tbs. salad oil
- 1 tbs. sugar
- 1 tbs. shoyu

- 5 eggs
- ½ tsp. salt
- 1 tbs. sake
- 1 tbs. salad oil for frying

Meat Wrapped in Eggs

PREPARATION

Split the fillets and then cut them up into small pieces. Cut the carrot into bits and cut the mushrooms into thin slices. Mince the leek starting from the edge.

Heat 2 tablespoons of salad oil in a frying pan and put the chicken, carrot, mushrooms, and leek in to fry one after the other. Sprinkle the sugar and the shoyu over the top and fry until steam stops rising.

Break and mix the eggs into a large bowl adding the sake and salt. Put the fried meat and vegetables in the bowl with the eggs and mix well.

In another frying pan heat one tablespoon of salad oil and when the oil covers the bottom of the pan pour the egg mixture into the pan. Fry over a flame which is between high and medium mixing all the time with a fork. Fry the eggs until they have hardened to the point where they are still slightly soft.

Finally sprinkle the green peas over the scrambled eggs. In place of chicken you may use ground beef or pork also.

leeks

isinglass

dried kelp strips

ginger roots

giant white Japanese radish

Beef and Veal Dishes

Meat Miso Sandwich, Boiled Eggplant and Ground Beef, Shoyu Steak, Boiled Veal Rolls

Meat Miso Sandwich

A soybean paste is spread on meat which is then folded over like a sandwich. This is then dusted in bread crumbs and fried. In place of veal, beef or pork can also be used.

INGREDIENTS (270 cal.)
    4 slices veal about 3½ oz. each
    3½ oz. miso
    2 tbs. sugar
    1 tsp. grated ginger root
    1 egg
    flour
    bread crumbs
    cooking oil
PREPARATION
Divide each veal piece into 2 slices cutting from the side. Mix the miso, sugar, ginger, and one egg yolk. Put this in between 2 slices of meat as though you were making a sandwich. Dust the meat "sandwich" with flour completely and dip it into the egg white. Now bread it with the crumbs.

Heat the cooking oil in a frying pan on a medium flame and fry the meat until it is all brown. Drain the oil off and cut into bite-size. This goes well with a fresh vegetable salad.

Boiled Eggplant and Ground Beef

In Japan eggplants are about the size of eggs or a little bigger. If the eggplants in your area are much larger than this it will improve the taste and shorten the cooking time if you deep fry them in oil before boiling.

INGREDIENTS (280 cal.)
    2 eggplants
    enough oil for frying
    1 lb. ground beef
    ⅓ of a chopped onion
    1 tbs. shoyu
    2 cups water
    4 tbs. shoyu
    8 tbs. sugar (if you have mirin use 7 tbs. instead of the sugar.)
    small amt. grated ginger root for garnish
PREPARATION
Remove the eggplant stems and peel them as shown in the illustration. Then *quickly* deep fry them in oil making certain they turn while frying. Then cut them into 1¼ in. lengths. Knead the chopped onion, ground beef with 1 tablespoon of shoyu thoroughly.

Put the water, shoyu, sugar (or use the mirin instead if you can), into a pot together with the fried eggplants and ground meat and slowly bring to a boil over a medium flame.

Serve each person at least 2 pieces of eggplants and over that spread the meat and other ingredients. Garnish with the grated ginger.

Peel the eggplant leaving the skin in strips as shown.

Shoyu Steak

Shoyu Steak

A delicious steak with a shoyu flavor. It can be served with any other foods although here we have used glazed carrots and broccoli.

INGREDIENTS (186 cal.)

    4 beef steaks
    3 tbs. shoyu
    1 tbs. sake
    1 tbs. mirin (1 tsp. sugar can be substituted)
    ½ tbs. vinegar
    1 tbs. salad oil
    2 tsp. grated ginger root
    1 kernel garlic
    1 tbs. butter for frying

PREPARATION

Soften and shape the meat by beating it with a tenderizer cutting all the sinews.

Make the marinade by putting the shoyu, sake, mirin, vinegar, salad oil, grated ginger and the garlic all together in a bowl. Mix well.

Pour this over the meat about 30 minutes before frying.

When ready to fry drain the meat thoroughly and then fry in the butter as you would any other steak.

Boiled Veal Rolls

In this dish veal is wrapped around vegetables and boiled with shoyu. Knives are not used at the dining table in Japan so the meat rolls are cut into bite sized pieces before serving.

INGREDIENTS (180 cal.)

    4 broad flat thin slices of veal (about 3 oz. per slice)
    1 small carrot
    1 small onion
    8 string beans

    3 tbs. shoyu
    2 tbs. sugar

    1½ cup water
    ⅛ tsp. salt
    2 tsp. cornstarch
    1 bunch ginger root

PREPARATION

Tenderize the meat by pounding it out flat with a meat tenderizer.

Cut the carrot into match stick size bits and the onion into thin slices. Cut the string beans up the same way as the carrot.

Spread the meat out flat and put the cut carrot, onion, and the string beans on it. Pound the right and left edges of the meat flat and then roll it up. Keep it from unrolling with toothpicks or better, sew the roll with cotton thread.

Put the shoyu, sugar, salt, and water into a deep wide mouth pan and boil. Next put the thinly sliced ginger and the meat in and boil the "otoshibuta" method. (see illustration)

Boil the meat for about 30 minutes stirring occasionally to bring out the full flavor.

Cut each roll into 3 or 4 pieces and arrange them on the serving plate so they stand on end. Take the ginger out of the pan. Make a thick paste out of the cornstarch (with a little water) and then mix this with the leftover liquid. Spread this gravy over the top of the meat rolls and serve.

"Otoshibuta" method of boiling. A lid slightly too little for the pan is placed in the pan during the boiling. This way the liquid will completely cover the food and bring out the flavor.

Okinawan Dishes

Okinawan-style Pork Soup, Okinawan "Rafutei," Okinawan-style Pork and Tofu

Okinawan-style Pork Soup

If possible this soup should be made using pieces of pork with the bones still attached but it can be made just as well with the meat alone. If you wish you may substitute chicken. However, the fattier cuts should be used. As the name suggests this dish originally came from Okinawa.

INGREDIENTS (215 cal.)

    10½ oz. pork spareribs.
    5¼ oz. giant white Japanese radish
    16 in. length of dried kelp (not essential)
    2 tsp. salt
    1 tsp. shoyu

PREPARATION

If you have the dried kelp wipe it well with a wet cloth and then cut it into 4 in. lengths. Tie each length into a simple knot.

Peel the radish and cut into 1¼ in. thick slices. Boil the meat, as is, in some water and then skim the fat carefully from the surface of the water. When the meat has boiled thoroughly add the kelp (or artificial seasoning) and the radish and continue boiling until the ingredients are soft. When the liquid boils off to where only 6 cups are left add the salt and shoyu.

Take the meat out and cut into four pieces. Put the pieces into bowls along with the kelp and the radish slices. Pour the hot liquid over and serve.

Okinawan "Rafutei"

This is one of the most famous Okinawan dishes and all visitors to the island usually sample it at least once. We in the homeland also have a similar dish.

INGREDIENTS (948 cal.)

    1¾ lb. pork spareribs
    23 in. dried kelp (not essential)
    5 tbs. shoyu
    3 tbs. sake (or white wine)
    5 tbs. sugar
    ¾ oz. minced ginger root
    ½ head lettuce

PREPARATION

Cut the spareribs into four equal pieces. Put them in plenty of water and boil. Keep the flame at a medium heat and skim the fat from the top as necessary. If you have kelp wipe it with a damp cloth and cut into 6 in. lengths. Put it in with the meat and boil until the meat is tender enough to skewer. (If you have no kelp use artificial seasoning instead.) At this point add the shoyu, sake (or white wine), and the sugar. Continue boiling until the liquid has evaporated somewhat. Serve with the lettuce leaves and the minced ginger.

Okinawan-style Pork Soup

Okinawan-style Pork and Tofu

Here is another dish which originally developed in Okinawa and is called "Tofu-irichi." "Irichi" means "to fry" in the Okinawan dialect. Its popularity has spread to the homeland. Try this dish for lunch or dinner.

INGREDIENTS (503 cal.)

2 blocks tofu
2½ oz. carrots
10½ oz. pork spareribs
1 tbs. sugar
2 tbs. shoyu
½ tsp. salt
1 sliced leek
3 tbs. oil

PREPARATION

Wrap the tofu in a cloth and gently press the water out. Then starting from the end slice in ½ in. slices.

Cut the carrot into 1¼ in. long pieces.

Boil the spareribs in plenty of water for as long as necessary until the meat is soft. Then cut into ½ in. widths and 2 in. lengths.

Heat 1 tablespoon of oil in a pan and *quickly* without breaking the slices fry the tofu. (This may take a little practice.) When the tofu is slightly brown take it out of the pan and allow the moisture to drain away.

Now heat 2 tablespoons of oil in a pan and put the carrots, tofu, and the boiled spareribs in to fry. Season with the sugar, shoyu, and the salt. Remove from pan and garnish with the sliced leek before serving.

Okinawan "Rafutei"

Okinawan-style Pork and Tofu

26

Chicken Dishes

Fried Chicken and Green Peppers, Japanese-style Hamburger Steak, Chicken Steamed in Sake, Boiled Chicken, Boiled Meat Dumplings and Turnips, Shoyu Fried Chicken, Boiled Chicken and Vegetables, Deep Fried Chicken and Corn, Japanese-style Fried Chicken

Fried Chicken and Green Peppers

This dish is guaranteed to give an unusual taste to that old favorite fried chicken. It will appeal to those who enjoy the strong flavors of ginger and hot red pepper. There are quite a few ingredients but it is not that difficult to make.

INGREDIENTS (276 cal.)

- 1¼ lb. spring chicken
- 1 tbs. shoyu
- ½ tbs. sake
- 3 tbs. cornstarch
- frying oil

- 3 green peppers
- 1 hot red pepper
- 1 piece ginger root
- 1 tbs. salad oil
- 2 tbs. shoyu
- 1 tbs. sake
- 1 tsp. sugar
- 2 tbs. water
- 1 tsp. cornstarch

- ½ bundle chicory
- ½ lemon

PREPARATION (276 cal.)

With a butcher knife cut the chicken, bones and all, into slightly larger than bite-size pieces. Sprinkle the shoyu and sake on the meat to bring out the flavor. Let it set for about 15 minutes and then dust it in cornstarch. Cover the meat thoroughly.

Heat the frying oil over a medium flame and deep fry the chicken for a good 4 minutes so it is thoroughly done. However, if the flame is too high the meat will burn.

Remove the seeds from the green peppers and cut them into 1¼ inch pieces. Remove the seeds from the hot red pepper and cut it into circular slices. Peel the ginger and mince it.

Heat 1 tablespoon of salad oil in a frying pan and fry the green pepper, the hot red pepper, and the ginger for 30 seconds. Then put the deep fried chicken in along with the sake, shoyu, sugar, and the water. Stirring constantly, fry for 1 minute longer. If there is excessive liquid make a paste with a little water and cornstarch and put this in the pan to take up the liquid.

When finished frying spread the ingredients on plates with the chicory and lemon slices. Squeeze the lemon over the food before eating.

Japanese-style Hamburger Steak

We usually fry the meat for this dish in one piece and cut it up later but you can fry it just as you would with regular hamburger if you prefer.

INGREDIENTS (314 cal.)

- 1 lb. ground pork or chicken
- 1 egg
- 4 tbs. bread crumbs
- 2 tbs. cornstarch
- 1 tbs. sugar
- 2 tbs. shoyu
- ½ tbs. salt

- 2 tbs. shoyu
- 2 tbs. sugar

- cooking oil
- foil
- ½ bundle spinach
- 1 tbs. shoyu
- 1 tsp. mustard
- artificial seasoning

PREPARATION

Mix the ground meat in a bowl with the egg, bread crumbs, cornstarch, sugar, shoyu, and the salt. Knead until the meat is firm.

Spread some foil on the bottom of shallow

Chicken steamed in Sake

pan and pour some oil over it. Then spread the meat over the foil to a thickness of about ¾ inch. Spread some oil on the surface of the meat with the tip of a knife. Bake in an oven on a medium heat for about 20 minutes.

Next boil the shoyu and the sugar in a small pan until some of the liquid evaporates. With a brush paint this shoyu sauce onto the cooked meat to improve the taste. Cut the meat into 1½ inch squares and put on plates.

Boil the spinach quickly, cut it to size and squeeze out the excess moisture. Mix some shoyu and mustard paste to pour over the spinach. Serve together with the meat.

Chicken Steamed in Sake

There are several names for this dish in Japanese and one of them is "Hakata obi." This is because the dish when wrapped up in foil resembles the vertical stripes of obi made in Hakata. You'll find this dish a simple and pleasant surprise to serve at your next party.

INGREDIENTS (130 cal.)

    4 chicken drumsticks
    8 ¼ in. thick slices of lemon
    12 mushrooms
    5 tbs. shoyu
    5 tbs. sake (or white wine with a little water
        added)

PREPARATION

Remove the bones from the drumsticks and cut each drumstick into 3 parts.

Cut the stems from the mushrooms, wash the tops and slice into thin slices.

Mix the shoyu and the sake and soak the chicken and mushroom slices in it for about 15 minutes.

Cut four 12 in. square pieces of aluminum foil and wrap the meat, mushrooms and lemon slices up in it sandwich style. Put these foil balls on a frying screen and cook over a medium flame for about 7 to 8 minutes.

Remove from the foil and serve.

Boiled Chicken

Dishes that are cooked by boiling in a pot are comparatively new in Japan. Some 200 years ago foreign traders introduced chicken soup to the Japanese people at the port of Nagasaki and today you can find this and similar dishes all over the nation. This is a dish to be eaten "family-style" with everyone around the table and the pan in the center on a burner or hot plate.

INGREDIENTS (257 cal.)

    1 chicken
    10½ oz. giant white Japanese radish
    3½ oz. carrots
    5 leeks
    10 cups water

28

Boiled Chicken

Fried Chicken and Green Peppers

salt
5 tbs. sake (white wine may be substituted)
vinegared shoyu (2 parts shoyu to 10 parts vinegar)
small amt. chopped leeks
small amt. grated giant white radish
small amt. dried powdered hot red pepper (or chili pepper)

PREPARATION

Cut the chicken up bones and all into 1–1½ inch chunks and wash until the water remains clear.

In Japan we usually cut the radish and carrots with an apple corer to make attractive round slices but you can cut them any way you wish. The pieces should be about 1½ in. in diameter. Cut the leeks into 2 in. lengths. Put 10 cups of water in a large pot together with the chicken and heat. When the water boils skim the surface removing all oil. Then put the radish and carrots in, turn the flame down low and simmer for about 2 hours. When the ingredients are soft season with salt and sake. Now put everything into a pan that you can continue to heat on the dining table. Add the leek pieces and continue heating at the table. Everyone helps themselves from the pan and dips the food into the sauce of vinegared shoyu, grated radish, finely chopped leeks and chili pepper before eating.

Boiled Meat Dumplings and Turnips

The meatballs in this dish are not fried but boiled with turnips.

INGREDIENTS (145 cal.)

12¼ oz. chicken or pork
1 tbs. grated onion
½ egg
3 tbs. bread crumbs
2 tbs. cornstarch
⅓ tsp. salt
2 tsp. shoyu
2 tsp. sugar

2 cups soup stock (or water with artificial seasoning added)
⅔ tsp. salt
2 tsp. shoyu
2 tsp. sugar
8 small turnips
1¾ oz. string beans

PREPARATION

Put the ground meat into a bowl and add the grated onion, egg, bread crumbs, cornstarch, salt, shoyu, and the sugar. Keeping your hands wet, make meatballs of 1 inch in diameter. Leave about 1 inch of the stem on the turnips and wash well. If you use fresh peas in the pod remove the strings.

Heat the soup stock, salt, shoyu, and sugar to boiling. Slip the meatballs in and let boil. When they have hardened push them to the side and put the turnips in and put a lid on the pan. Simmer over a low flame for about

29

10 minutes. When the turnips are soft add the string beans and simmer for only one minute or so. Remove and serve before the string beans lose their color.

Shoyu Fried Chicken

Chicken is soaked in shoyu to which grated ginger has been added. If possible the meat should be cooked over a direct flame. This dish has a very light simple taste.

INGREDIENTS (175 cal.)

1 lb. chicken meat
4 tbs. shoyu
1 tbs. mirin or sake
2 tsp. grated ginger root
artificial seasoning
small amt. salad oil
1 stalk celery
1 cucumber
3 tbs. vinegar
1 tbs. sugar
½ tsp. salt
artificial seasoning

PREPARATION

Cut the chicken in to thin slices and sprinkle the shoyu, ginger, mirin (or sake), and the artificial seasoning over it. Let it sit for about 15 minutes so the flavor can develop.

With a brush paint a frying screen with salad oil and heat it. When hot enough put the chicken on one slice at a time and fry each side until slightly browned. The meat can also be fried in a pan with salad oil but much of the flavor of the shoyu will be lost.

Mince the celery cutting across the stalk. Cut the cucumber into little pieces the same way. Sprinkle some salt over both and let sit for 5 or 6 minutes. Then squeeze them in your hands to wring out the water. Put them in a bowl and mix with the vinegar,

sugar, salt, and the artificial seasoning. Serve together with the chicken.

Boiled Chicken and Vegetables

For this dish first fry the chicken and vegetables. Then boil them with shoyu. This is a very common dinner for families in Japan.

INGREDIENTS (264 cal.)

10½ oz. boneless chicken meat
2 carrots about 3½ in. lengths
3 potatoes medium size
2 bamboo shoots (the canned type)
4 green peppers
3 tbs. salad oil
½ cup water
2½ tbs. sugar
4 tbs. shoyu
artificial seasoning

PREPARATION

Cut the chicken meat into small pieces. Peel the potatoes and carrots; then chop into bite-size pieces. Cut the bamboo shoots in the same way. Cut the peppers in half, take out the seeds and cut the sections into about 6 pieces each. (see picture)

Heat the salad oil in a pan and first fry the chicken, then add the carrots, then the potatoes, and finally the bamboo shoots. Fry them all together thoroughly for about 4 minutes.

Now add the water, sugar, and the shoyu plus whatever other seasoning you wish. When it boils turn the flame down low and put a lid on the pan. Simmer until the vegetables are soft. Finally, add the peppers and stir until the liquid has evaporated.

Boiled Chicken and Vegetables

Japanese-style Fried Chicken

Deep Fried Chicken and Corn

The idea for this dish came from a tempura recipe using baby shrimp and tofu. In place of chicken meat you can use shrimp also if you wish. It is very tasty when served that way also.

INGREDIENTS (146 cal.)

  1 cup cut corn
  10½ oz. chicken meat
  small amt. cooking oil
  ½ cup crushed tofu
  1 egg
  ½ cup water
  1 cup or less flour
  frying oil
  ½ cup shoyu
  ½ cup water
  a little grated giant white radish
  a little grated ginger root

PREPARATION

Boil the cut corn in a pan. Cut the chicken meat into chunks about ½ in. in size and fry. Put this fried chicken in the pan with the corn, crushed tofu, egg, water, and the flour and mix well. Heat the frying oil to about 300 to 340 degrees F. and drop the mixture in to fry a spoonful at a time. Be careful not to burn it.

Mix the shoyu with about ½ cup water and then add the grated radish and ginger.

Put a little of this sauce on each bite you eat.

In order to absorb the excess cooking oil put a paper napkin on each plate before serving.

Japanese-style Fried Chicken

We have two ways of frying: one using flour and the other way using cornstarch. A good part of the chicken to use is the drumstick after the bone has been removed. However, it is not necessary to do this. As you see in the picture in Japan fried food is usually served with a folded paper napkin beneath it.

INGREDIENTS (133 cal.)

  4 chicken drumsticks
  8 tbs. shoyu
  small amt. sake (not essential)
  small amt. flour
  a little bit of lemon
  oil

PREPARATION

Slice the drumstick down along the leg in the same direction as the bone but not as deep as the bone. Cut each leg into 4 parts. Put the meat into a bowl and add the shoyu and sake and let soak for about 20 minutes. Then dust lightly in flour and fry gently in oil.

Fold a paper napkin onto each plate and place a slice of lemon to the side. We sometimes use mustard also. Eat while still warm.

Japanese Soy Sauce — Shoyu

Shoyu is the single seasoning without which the art of Japanese cooking would be impossible. Its flavor and fragrance also blend beautifully with food of other countries, and shoyu is now in use throughout the world. Japan's largest shoyu producer, the Kikkoman Shoyu Company, exports its product to 51 countries around the world.

The most important ingredient in cooking is, of course, flavor. And one reason advanced to explain the popularity of shoyu in countries other than Japan is that its unique flavor and fragrance offer something special to all who have been caught up in the age of "instant foods." It is undeniable that instant foods are convenient, and equally undeniable that most of them need the kind of taste brightening that shoyu does so well. However, it is especially in home cooking that shoyu is being used to create new taste treats and surprises in Western dishes. There is no doubt that the use of shoyu in kitchens and on dining tables throughout the world will continue to grow.

But before we go any further let us take a closer look at this seasoning called shoyu. First of all, how did it develop and what is its relationship to Japanese cooking?

Oceans surround Japan in all four directions and the four seasons of the year are clearly distinguishable. Thus the country is blessed with both fresh sea foods and plentiful farm products. The traditional characteristics of Japanese cooking are: simplicity of taste, quiet elegance, visual beauty and attention to detail.

Modern Japanese cooking, as compared to traditional cooking, shows both the influences of the entire Orient plus the Occident, together with the changes that the younger generation has brought about. However, in spite of these many changes, the best of the traditional methods can still be found even today. Among these traditional methods the influence of Buddhism was especially strong in regard to developing a respect for the natural flavor of each food item. The best means of bringing out the flavor of each food was found to be through the use of shoyu.

This soy sauce is also made in China but the raw materials, production method, color, and fragrance are entirely different from Japanese shoyu. Consequently, Chinese soy sauce is not used in preparing Japanese foods.

It is believed that some time in the distant past shoyu was accidentally discovered through the method then used for preserving protein foods, such as fish, fowl, and other meats. These foods were cured in salt and the liquid which accumulated in the process was found to be rather sweet, and so it came to be used as a seasoning.

Thus the first raw materials for the production of shoyu seem to have been meats, but gradually a change to various beans and grains came about. It is said that this was due to the Buddhist teachings forbidding the killing of animals but actually it seems more likely that beans produced a tastier seasoning than meats.

Scientifically speaking, this is because when protein undergoes chemical decomposition some 20 kinds of amino acids are produced—all with various tastes. Animal protein alone in the same process produces bad smelling chemicals (such as ammonia) and amino acids of bad taste. The use of raw materials such as soybeans and wheat produces a liquid which contains large amounts of pleasant tasting, fragrant chemicals, such as glutamic acid, glycine, alcohol, lactic acid, and acetic acid. This method of making seasoning from soybeans and wheat underwent great development in Japan, and the result is modern shoyu. In Japan equal amounts of soybeans and wheat are used in shoyu production, whereas in China mostly soybeans are used. The starch contained in the wheat is acted upon by yeast to become a sugary substance and this in turn through fermentation and lactation produces alcohol, lactic acid, and acetic acid. This combination of alcohol and acids gives Japanese shoyu its uniquely fine flavor. Similarly, the reason that wines are used as seasoning in Western dishes is that the alcohol brings out the sweetness of the foods, as does shoyu. It is also said that alcohol helps heat penetrate into foods.

As can be seen from the above, the flavor of shoyu depends upon the raw materials used. Shoyu flavor and quality also depend upon production methods. There are two production methods: one is natural brewing and the other is chemical production.

Pure Japanese shoyu is naturally brewed, and the longer the fermentation period the more savory the shoyu becomes. The clear reddish-black color of Japanese shoyu is the result of the use of high quality raw materials and a long fermentation period.

Shoyu produced by the Kikkoman Company is aged for a year and a half to bring out the flavor of the natural fermentation process. The shoyu that results from this natural method has countless ingredients acting upon each other, which creates the finest natural flavor.

On the other hand, virtually all Chinese soy sauce is produced chemically (by hydrochlorination), and it includes additives such as corn syrup and caramel coloring. This chemical method relies upon a chemical reaction between hydrochloric acid and protein. It takes only a short time, and thus produces a very low-cost product. The amino acids, however, which result from the decomposition of chlorine go through further extreme decomposition which may have adverse effects on the quality of the product. Although Chinese soy sauce has some of the sweetness of the amino acids, it does not have the flavor of alcohol or the other acids. Consequently, Chinese soy sauce if used in Japanese cooking would destroy the taste. One can usually tell the difference by simply comparing the color—Chinese soy sauce will be much blacker and denser than Japanese shoyu. The most eloquent testimony for the comparative quality of Japanese shoyu is the fact that it is used in most of the better Chinese restaurants outside China.

But now let us take a look at how shoyu is used in Japanese cooking. It is most commonly found in sukiyaki, teriyaki, and tempura. It is also used with boiled meats, fish, and vegetables, and in various soups. As a seasoning on the dining table, although salt is almost never found on Japanese dining tables, shoyu always is. It complements sliced fresh fish, fried eggs, broiled fish, pickled vegetables and is used as the main ingredient in various sauces—some of which are given in this book. In Western cooking shoyu is commonly used with virtually any kind of meat dish, fried, broiled, boiled or stewed. It is also used with fish, soups and casseroles. On the dining table it flavors foods such as ham and eggs, omelets, and other egg dishes. It is delicious sprinkled over almost any meat or fried fish dish. It also improves the taste of fried vegetables.

The lists above do not begin to cover all the areas where shoyu can be creatively used. There are countless dishes which come alive with the simple addition of shoyu. Mixing shoyu with mayonnaise and other dressings for salads, for example, will result in a truly surprising taste change for the better.

Finally, here are some suggestions for the use of shoyu. Although shoyu will keep for a long time, avoid leaving it near hot stoves, etc. Refrigeration is the ideal method of storage. Only buy as much as you will use in two or three weeks time to ensure the freshest flavor.

All the delightful taste treats of shoyu cooking await you in this book. We feel certain that many readers will come to find it as indispensable in cooking and seasoning as millions of other homemakers and cooks already have.

Pork Dishes

Meatballs Steamed with Rice, Boiled Pork, Tempura-type Pork, Pork Cutlets Japanese-style, Boiled Pork and Potatoes, Roast Pork, Steamed Cabbage Leaves Wrapped around Ground Pork, Marinated Pork, Fried Eggplant and Ground Meat Sandwich-style

Meatballs steamed with Rice

Meatballs Steamed with Rice

Here's one of the most interesting way to serve meat and rice that anyone could imagine. And the taste is really delightful. However, don't forget that the rice has to soak quite a while.

INGREDIENTS (362 cal.)

    14 oz. ground pork
    1 tbs. shoyu
    ⅔ tsp. salt
    1 tsp. sugar
    1 medium size chopped onion
    1 tsp. grated ginger root
    3 tbs. flour
    artificial seasoning
    ⅔ cup glutinous rice or regular rice

PREPARATION

Soak the rice in water overnight. (The rice will expand so use a pan big enough.) Drain well. (If you want to shorten the soaking time use lukewarm water.)

Mix the ground meat with the shoyu, salt, sugar, chopped onion, grated ginger, flour and the artificial seasoning in a bowl. Knead until the meat becomes firm.

Spread the rice onto a tray. Form the meat into balls about plum size. Roll these in the rice so the rice covers them. Spread a wet cloth in a steamer that is giving off steam and put the meatballs on it. Steam for about 20 minutes. Eat while still hot; dipping the meatballs into the mixed mustard and shoyu.

Boiled Pork

A dish with a simple taste eaten with a mustard shoyu sauce.

INGREDIENTS (770 cal.)

    1½ lb. pork roast
    2½ cups water
    ½ cup sake
    1 tsp. salt
    1 leek or onion
    ginger root

    10½ oz. Brussels sprouts
    2 tbs. vinegar
    2 tbs. shoyu
    small amt. sugar
    ½ tbs. salad oil or sesame oil
    1 tsp. mustard
    artificial seasoning

PREPARATION

Roll the pork up with the fat toward the outside and tie with strong string.

In a deep pan add the water, sake, salt, meat, leek (cut to fit pan), or onion (cut in half), and ginger (peel and mash with shaft of butcher knife). Heat over a high flame with no lid on pan. Skim the surface as necessary with a spoon. When the liquid clears put the lid on and boil for 30 minutes.

Score the bottom of the Brussels sprouts and boil for 3 to 4 minutes in water to which a little salt has been added. Then drain. Mix the vinegar, shoyu, sugar, salad oil (or sesame oil), mustard, and the artificial seasoning. Put the Brussels sprouts into this to be seasoned.

After the boiled pork has cooled somewhat remove the strings, slice from the end in thin slices and serve together with the Brussels sprouts. Eat the meat with a little mustard mixed with shoyu on each piece if desired. The leftover liquid which the meat was boiled in can be used for cooking other dishes.

Tempura-type Pork

Pork soaked in shoyu sauce and cooked tempura-style. An unusual dinner dish.

INGREDIENTS (440 cal.)

- 14 oz. pork (thinly sliced)
- 3 tbs. shoyu
- 1 tbs. cooking oil
- ½ tbs. sugar
- 1 piece ginger root
- 1 kernel garlic

- 1 egg
- 3 tbs. water
- 4 tbs. cornstarch
- ¼ tsp. salt
- cooking oil
- 1 leek

PREPARATION

Cut the pork into bite-size. Sprinkle the shoyu, cooking oil, sugar, grated ginger, and the chopped garlic on the meat and rub it in.

Break and mix the egg. Make a paste of the cornstarch with a little water and add the salt. Mix well with the egg. Cut the leek into 1½ in. lengths. Remove the cores. Cut the outer skin open and then into ⅛ in. wide strips. Wrap the strips in a cloth and hold under cold running water. Squeeze the excess water out and unwrap. (see illustration)

Heat the cooking oil over a medium flame. Drain excess seasoning sauce from the meat and cover it with the cornstarch paste. Fry to where the color changes to light brown. Wrap the leek strips in a cloth and squeeze the water out. Sprinkle the curly leek strips on top of the fried meat.

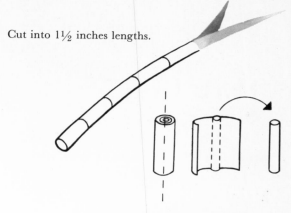

Cut into 1½ inches lengths.

Cut lengthwise half way thru then remove the core.

Spread the outer skin flat and slice as shown.

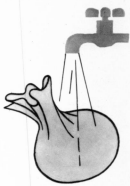

Wrap the slices in a cloth and rinse under cold water.

The leek strips will curl as shown.

Pork Cutlets Japanese-style

Pork cutlets, of course, are originally a Western dish but it has now become a Japanese dish also. In Japan it is always served with chopped cabbage and a meat sauce.

INGREDIENTS (616 cal.)

- 4 slices of fatless pork about 5¼ oz. each slice
- small amt. salt and pepper
- flour
- 1 egg
- bread crumbs
- cooking oil
- several cabbage leaves
- meat sauce

PREPARATION

Beat the meat out flat with a tenderizer cutting all the sinews. Sprinkle on salt and pepper and let sit for 5 to 6 minutes.

Cover each slice lightly with flour and dip it in the egg. Bread thoroughly with the crumbs and let sit for 3 minutes.

Heat plenty of cooking oil and put each slice in one at a time to fry for about 3 minutes. When the surface is light brown remove and drain the oil off.

Chop the cabbage fine and serve with the meat and meat sauce.

You can also cut the pork into 1 in. thick pieces and bread the same way and then cook it on a skewer stick 3 pieces at a time.

Boiled Pork and Potatoes

When meat is boiled slowly for a long time as with this dish the fat seems to get soft and melt. This dish uses a kind of sweet and sour cooking method.

INGREDIENTS (956 cal.)

- 1½ lb. pork peices
- 1 tbs. salad oil
- 3 tbs. sugar
- 1 piece ginger root
- 4 cups water
- ⅓ cup sake
- 2 tbs. sugar
- ½ tsp. salt
- 4 tbs. shoyu
- 4 small potatoes
- 1 leek
- mustard

PREPARATION

Cut the pork into 3 in. square pieces. Heat the cooking oil and the sugar in a frying pan and when it turns a caramel color put the pork and the thinly sliced ginger in. Make sure the meat is completely covered with this liquid and is a brown color.

Next pour the contents of the frying pan into a deep pan and add the water, sake, sugar, salt, and the shoyu.

Simmer on a very low flame for about an hour and a half. (Add a little more water if it becomes necessary.)

Cut the potatoes into small round pieces and put them in to simmer after the meat becomes soft.

Cut the leek to about 1½ in. lengths and remove the cores. Then cut the leek into strips as shown in the illustration below.

When both the meat and potatoes are soft pour the contents of the pan into a deep bowl and sprinkle the curly leek strips on top of the meat before serving.

Roast Pork

This is a type of Japanese-style roast pork. The meat is soaked for several hours in shoyu and then fried. If you have any leftover it goes good in lunch boxes or sandwiches or even fried rice.

INGREDIENTS (730 cal.)

- 1½–2 lb. pork loin
- ⅔ cup shoyu
- 3 tbs. sake
- 3 tbs. sugar
- 2 leeks
- 1 piece ginger root

PREPARATION

Cut the pork so that it is about 3 in. in diameter and then wrap it with a string as you would for a roast. (see picture)

Put the shoyu, sake, sugar, finely cut leeks, and the thinly cut ginger into a bowl. Mix well. Put the meat in and let sit for 4 to 5 hours turning occasionally.

Heat the oven to a medium heat and put a roasting screen over a flat shallow pan. Put the meat on the screen and roast for about 40 minutes. Baste with a brush 4 or 5 times while roasting. When the whole roast takes on a good color it should be done.

After removing from the oven do not take the strings off for about 10 minutes. Slice thinly and serve. The basting sauce can be heated and served with the meat as a kind of gravy.

Steamed Cabbage Leaves Wrapped around Ground Pork

This dish can be steamed in a deep pan but we usually put the ingredients into a square container and put this container into a steamer to steam over a high flame for about 40 minutes. When cooked this way no shoyu is added. After steaming it is cut into individual portions and eaten with a sauce of mustard and shoyu. If a lot of people are going to eat you can use a large pot and instead of steaming boil slowly over a low flame.

INGREDIENTS (285 cal.)

6 cabbage leaves
{ 12¼ oz. ground pork
  ½ chopped onion
  1 tsp. salt
  small amt. pepper
  1 tsp. shoyu
{ 2 cups water
  2 tbs. shoyu
  mustard-shoyu sauce (2 tbs. mustard and 4 tbs. shoyu)

PREPARATION

Knead the ground pork, chopped onion, salt, pepper, and the shoyu all together.

Boil the cabbage leaves very quickly, cut out the stems and squeeze the excess water out.

Put two cabbage leaves in the bottom of a 5 in. deep pan and spread the meat on top of the leaves. On top of this spread the remaining leaves in overlapping fasion and cut an "X" down from the top all the way to the bottom with a knife.

Add 2 cups of water, 2 tablespoons of shoyu

Steamer

and heat over a low flame until the liquid evaporates. Remove with a spatula and serve. Dip each bite into the mustard-shoyu sauce before eating.

Marinated Pork

This is another dish which originally was brought to Japan by the Portuguese and Spanish traders. Over the years it has developed a Japanese flavor but we still call it "Marinated Pork Foreign-style." This recipe is delicious with either fish or chicken also.

INGREDIENTS (454 cal.)

{ 1¼ lb. pork
  small amt. shoyu to flavor the meat
{ 10 leeks
  1 cup vinegar
  2 tbs. shoyu
  4 tbs. water
  ½ tsp. salt
  1½ tbs. sugar
  small amt. cornstarch
  oil
  small amt. dried red pepper (or chili pepper)

PREPARATION

Slice the pork into thin ½ in. slices thick and bite-size length. Marinate in shoyu for about 10 minutes.

Fry the leeks, as is, until they are only slightly brown and then cut them into 1¼ in. lengths. Mix the vinegar, shoyu, water, salt, and the sugar together and marinate the fried leeks in this. Drain the excess shoyu off the marinated pork and then dust lightly with the cornstarch. Deep fry the pork thoroughly in oil heated to 340 degrees F. Then marinate it once more while it is still hot in the marinate sauce. Sprinkle some finely chopped red pepper (or chili pepper) over the top and let soak for about 40 minutes.

Drain the marinate off; remove the leeks from the sauce and serve the leeks with the meat as garnish.

Fried Eggplant and Ground Meat Sandwich-style

With this dish the ground meat is sandwiched in between the eggplant and fried. If your eggplants are too large you'll have to cut them down to the right size.

INGREDIENTS (270 cal.)

- 4 eggplants (less if they are large)
- 7 oz. ground pork
- 3 tbs. chopped onion
- 1 tbs. shoyu
- ½ tbs. sugar
- ½ egg
- 3 tbs. water
- 5 tbs. flour
- ½ egg
- small amt. salt
- oil for frying
- shoyu or meat sauce

PREPARATION

Peel the eggplant and cut it into ½ in. thick circular slices. Soak the slices in water for about 15 minutes then drain-well. Mix the ground pork, egg, chopped onion, shoyu, and the sugar. Using the eggplant slices as bread make sandwiches with the ground meat. Dust the inner surface of the eggplant with flour before making the sandwich.

Next make the outer paste with the ½ egg mixed well and thinned a little with water. Add the flour and salt and mix well. Heat the oil in a pan over a medium flame. Cover the eggplant sandwich with the paste and deep fry it. Drain the excess oil and place the sandwiches on plates. Put a folded paper napkin on the plate to absorb the leftover oil. Put some shoyu or meat sauce in a small dish and dip the "swandwich" into it before each bite.

MODERN JAPANESE COOKING

Although it is only natural that we Japanese people enjoy our traditional foods and cooking methods nevertheless, we still eat foreign foods often and with gusto. Especially in the post-war period contact with foreign countries has increased and this has stimulated changes in the eating habits of the people. This is particularly true in the cities where families eating strictly Japanese-style food three meals a day are rare indeed. Many families now have breakfasts of toast, fried eggs, and coffee. Even families who still eat the traditional Japanese breakfast of rice, miso soup, and Japanese pickles will probably have spaghetti or macaroni or some other Western dish for lunch and/or dinner. Younger Japanese seem to be very fond of high calorie Western cooking whereas older Japanese seem to prefer the comparatively low calorie simple traditional foods.

Certain dishes which are now considered to be part of Japanese cooking actually were introduced from abroad. For example, curry, pork cutlets, stew, croquettes, and many others are generally considered to be "Japanese-style" foods. Curry rice is to be found in even the smallest countryside restaurant and pork cutlets and croquettes are sold already cooked for housewives to take home.

Various kinds of stews are very popular and have taken on certain Japanese touches. Not only have Western foods been completely adopted by the people but an dexterity at skilfully mixing traditional and imported dishes has developed. For example, the following mixed menu is very common and natural: Japanese-style soup, beefsteak, boiled spinach with dressing (in place of salad), and rice with Japanese pickles. In this way cooks are able to combine a Western-style main dish, whether it is meat or fish, with complimentary Japanese dishes to complete the menu for the meal. On the other hand, should a cook in a Western country put a Japanese dish in the menu it would doubtless come as quite a surprise in most households. This is certainly one way of enlivening a jaded menu and the possibilities are almost endless. A clear Japanese suimono in place of soup; Japanese-style meat or fish dishes; or in place of the ordinary salad why not one done Japanese-style. Should Japanese cooking come to be regularly used in Western countries appreciation of its delicacy, simplicity, and beauty will doubtless make it very popular. Japanese cooking is a part of our people and country and we are grateful for the opportunity to teach it to you.

Canned Foods and Salads

Canned Salmon and Egg over Rice, Chicken, Crab and Vegetables with Vinegared Shoyu Sauce, Crab Omelet, Japanese-style Salad

Canned Salmon and Egg over Rice

For this dish we recommend that you use canned red salmon as the color will be very pleasing. However, if you don't mind the color you may also use canned tuna.

INGREDIENTS (253 cal.)

{ 1 can red salmon
1 tsp. sake
2 tbs. sugar
¼ tsp. salt

{ 4 eggs
2 tbs. sugar
¼ tsp. salt
1 tbs. sake

{ 4 cups cooked rice
small amt. kidney beans

PREPARATION

Drain the canned salmon well and remove all skin and bones. Put into a small pan and break the meat into pieces. Add the sake, sugar and the salt and while mixing well with a fork heat until no liquid remains.

Break the eggs into a small pan and add the sugar, salt, and the sake. Repeat the same heating process just as above. Continue mixing until thoroughly cooked. Be sure to use a low flame or the eggs will stick to the pan bottom.

Put the red salmon and the yellow eggs on top of the rice keeping the colors separated. Boil the kidney beans in some water with salt and after mincing sprinkle them over the top and serve.

How To Cook Rice

(We recommend that you cook the rice rather than use a "pre-cooked" variety. It is not difficult and there is no comparison in taste.) Wash 1½ cups of rice in cold water and

Canned Salmon and Egg over Rice

drain well. Put the washed rice into a thick deep pot together with 1⅔ cups water. Put the lid on and start heating with a strong flame. As the rice boils turn the flame down so that it does not boil over. Keep the flame at this strength for 3 minutes and then turn the flame down low for 15 minutes. Now turn the flame off and let set for 10 minutes. The amount of water necessary varies with the type of rice you use and where the rice was grown but generally about 20% more water than rice is recommended.

Chicken, Crab and Vegetables with Vinegared Shoyu Sauce

Here's a hint: if you have sesame seed oil pour 1 tablespoon over the ingredients just before serving for an added taste treat.

INGREDIENTS (199 cal.)

1 onion
1¼ in. carrot
1 cucumber
10½ oz. chicken
1 can crab meat
5 tbs. sake (or white wine or water)
1 tsp. salt
small amt. pepper
- 4 tbs. chicken soup stock
- 6 tbs. shoyu
- 2½ tbs. vinegar
- 2 tsp. ginger root

PREPARATION

Cut the onion in half and then into thin slices. Soak them in water for about 15 minutes to remove the sharpness.

Slice the carrot up and peel the cucumber. Remove the cucumber seeds and cut the remainder up into little peices. Soak in water.

Cut the chicken into large chunks and fry well using the sake, salt, and the pepper. Then cut the chunks into slices. Squeeze the excess moisture out of the vegetables. Spread the crab meat out and remove all bones. Mix all ingredients together. Mix the 4 tablespoons of chicken stock with the shoyu, vinegar, and the ginger paste for your sauce. Put the chicken, crab meat and the vegetables on plates and pour the sauce over just before eating.

Crab Omelet

Originally this was a Chinese-style crab and egg omelet but it has come to be a common dish on Japanese dinner tables and consequently the taste has taken on more of a Japanese flavor.

INGREDIENTS (210 cal.)

- 1 can crab meat
- 1 leek (or 1 small onion diced)
- 2 tsp. finely chopped parsley
- 1 tbs. salad oil
- ⅓ tsp. salt
- 1 tsp. salt
- 6 eggs
- 1 tbs. salad oil for frying
- ½ cup soup stock or water
- 1 tbs. shoyu
- 1 tbs. sake
- 2 tsp. sugar
- 1 tbs. grated ginger root
- 2 tsp. cornstarch

PREPARATION

Remove all bones from the crab and squeeze the moisture out. Then spread the meat out.

Heat 1 tablespoon of salad oil in a frying pan and fry the finely sliced leek (or the chopped onion). Add ⅓ teaspoon of salt, 1 teaspoon of sugar and the chopped parsley by sprinkling lightly over the leeks.

Break the eggs into a bowl and mix in the fried leeks and the crab meat. Wash the frying pan and heat it again. Put in 1 tablespoon of salad oil and when this has covered the bottom of the pan pour all the egg mixture into the pan. When it has hardened somewhat stir the ingredients around then cover the pan and turn the flame down low. Fry until hardened. Turn the omelet over and cook on the other side for about one minute. Heat the soup stock or water in a small pot together with the shoyu, sake, sugar, and the artificial seasoning. Make a thick paste of the cornstarch with a little water and when the water has about boiled pour the paste in together with the grated ginger.

Put the crab meat omelet on a plate and pour this paste over the top. Divide into individual portions and serve.

Crab Omelet

44

Japanese-style Salad

Western vegetables are used in this salad but the dressings are Japanese.

INGREDIENTS (40 cal.)

½ bundle chicory
3 lettuce leaves
1 stick celery
1 cucumber
1 tomato
3 leaves red cabbage
some watercress and leeks

Miso dressing (in the yellow dish on the far left)

4 tbs. miso
2 tbs. sugar
1–1½ tsp. mustard paste
2–3 tbs. vinegar

Japanese-style mayonnaise (in the red dish second from the left)

1 egg yolk
3 tbs. vinegar
1 tbs. mirin or sake
1 tbs. sugar
½ tsp. salt

Vinegared shoyu dressing (in the green dish third from the left)

3 tbs. vinegar
1–1½ tbs. shoyu
½ tsp. salt

Peanut butter dressing (in the blue dish on the right)

3 tbs. vinegar
1 tbs. sugar

Japanese-style Salad

⅔ tsp. salt
2 tbs. peanut butter

PREPARATION

Prepare the vegetables in the same way as for a Western salad. After washing shake excess moisture off and put the vegetables into a bowl. Cut the leek into about 2 in. lengths. To make the flower in the picture cut a 2 in. length of leek and make perpendicular cuts into the top of the stalk. Soak it in cold water and these "petals" will open. (see illustation)

For the miso dressing put the miso and sugar in a small pan and knead it while heating. After it softens turn off the heat and mix it with the mustard paste and vinegar.

To make the Japanese-style mayonnaise put the egg yolk into a bowl. Heat the vinegar, mirin (or sake), sugar, and salt in a small pan. Then pour it in with the egg yolk and mix quickly. Float the bowl in very hot water and mix the dressing until it "melts" into a soft consistency. Cool before use.

The vinegared shoyu dressing is simply made by just thoroughly mixing the vinegar, shoyu, and the salt. The same amount of salad oil as that of vinegar can be added according to taste.

The peanut butter dressing is made by mixing the vinegar, sugar, salt and the peanut butter in a small bowl with a mixer.

Any of these dressings can be used with salad according to individual taste.

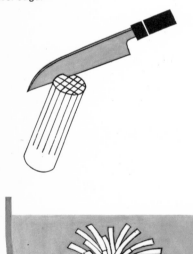

Making the "flower."

Desserts

Mixed Fruit and Isinglass, Solid "Snow" Dessert, Tea Napkin Shaped Sweet Potato Balls, "Yellow Flower" Dessert, Milk Jelly and Mixed Fruit, Steamed Castile Cake

Mixed Fruit and isinglass

Mixed Fruit and Isinglass

In Japan we use many desserts which call for a kind of gelatine which is actually isinglass or Japanese isinglass. Isinglass is made from a kind of seaweed called "heaven grass" and it contains no calories. Dieting women often use it. There are 3 types or shapes:

long and stick-like, rope-like, and powdered. However, the stick-like type is probably the easiest to measure. It is said that it coagulates 10 times better than gelatine and there is no need to refrigerate it as it will harden even at room temperature.

INGREDIENTS (192 cal.)

1 stick Japanese isinglass
2 cups water
½ cup boiled red sweet beans (available in cans)
4 slices canned pineapple
1 small can mandarin oranges
4 yellow peach slices
a few cherries
1 cup sugar
⅓ cup water

PREPARATION

Break the isinglass into pieces and soak for 30 minutes in water. When it has soaked thoroughly squeeze all the water out and put it in a pan. Add 2 cups of water and heat, stirring all the while. After boiling pour the liquid into an empty tin can or small metal pan after first wetting the sides of the container. Let set until hard. (If you are in a

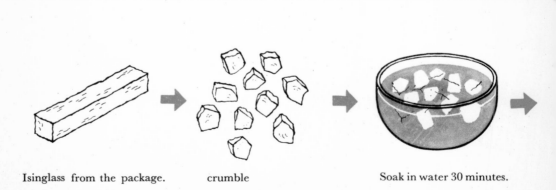

Isinglass from the package.   crumble   Soak in water 30 minutes.

hurry you can put it in your refrigerator.) Then remove it and cut into ½ inch squares. Remove any pits from the canned fruit and cut the fruit into small chunks. If you use canned red sweet beans drain well and then pour hot water over them and cool. If you have fresh beans soak them overnight in water and then boil gently adding a little salt just before removing from the heat.

Heat the cup of sugar in ¼ cup water and then cool this syrup. Mix the isinglass, fruit, and beans in a glass bowl and pour the syrup over the top. Serve chilled.

Solid "Snow" Dessert

Solid "Snow" Dessert

Here is a dessert with a very simple taste and a simple white color to match.

INGREDIENTS (60 cal.)

    1 stick Japanese isinglass
    1½ cup water
    6 tbs. sugar
    small amt. grated lemon peel
    2 egg whites

PREPARATION

Soak the isinglass (after breaking it into medium size chunks) the same way you soaked the sweet beans. Then squeeze the water out and boil in 1½ cup water. Add half of the sugar (3 tbs.) and when the sugar has melted remove from the heat and allow to cool.

Put the egg whites into a dry bowl and after adding a very little bit of salt beat with an egg beater. Gradually add the remaining 3 tbs. of sugar and continue to beat rapidly. This

way the dessert texture becomes soft and smooth. Now pour the still warm isinglass mixture gradually into the beaten egg whites mixing as you do so. (If the mixture is too hot the egg whites will not mix with it and it will turn out in layers.) Then pour this combination into a wet empty can and allow to harden. Cut into appropriate size servings. Here we cut a strawberry in half and placed it on the top but a fruit syrup or honey will also do nicely.

Tea Napkin Shaped Sweet Potato Balls

For this recipe you'll need some white cotton cloths to boil the potato slices in and to shape them later. This is a dessert we often serve at parties in Japan.

Add two cups of water.

Squeeze water out.

Boil until isinglass completely dissolves.

Tea Napkin Shaped Sweet Potato Balls

INGREDIENTS (284 cal.)

1 lb. sweet potatoes
4 tbs. sugar
small amt. salt
8 sweet boiled chestnuts

PREPARATION

Peel the potatoes cutting a little deeply into the skin. Then slice into very thin round slices and wash until the water remains clear. This way the color of the potatoes will turn out appetizing. Drain the excess water from the slices. Put a wet cloth in the bottom of a steamer which has boiling water in it. Then put the slices in and finally another cloth on top. Boil on a high flame for 5 to 6 minutes or until the potatoes are soft. Then before the potatoes cool grate or mash them adding the sugar and salt. Next using a masher continue kneading in a pan over a low flame for 3 or 4 minutes. At this point you can, if you wish, add some butter or brandy or vanila which will improve the taste as well as the fragrance.

Now divide the potatoes into 8 round ball shaped portions with each portion having a diameter of 1¼ inches. Put the portions on a wet cloth and push a chestnut down into the center of the top. Then wrap the cloth around the portion and squeeze it into the shape as shown in the illustration.

"Yellow Flower" Dessert

This dish, made with the white and the yolk of the egg, is yellow-white and it resembles a "yellow flower." The dish, made with the white of the egg only, is white and because it then resembles the snow which falls just before spring we call it "spring snow."

INGREDIENTS (39 cal.)

2½ gelatin blocks
⅓ cup water
2 egg whites
2 egg yolks
1 cup sugar
1 cup water

PREPARATION

Boil the gelatin blocks in ⅓ cup of water for about 20 minutes.

Beat the 2 egg whites until they are firm. Mix the cup of water and the cup of sugar and heat so the sugar dissolves. Take it off the heat when about ⅓ of the mixture has boiled off and when the remainder has cooled some

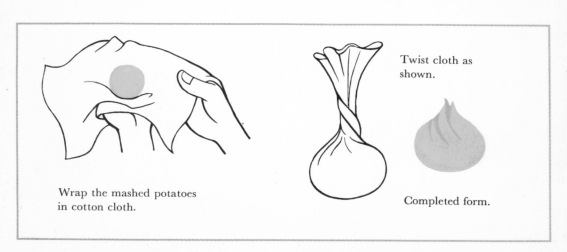

Wrap the mashed potatoes in cotton cloth.

Twist cloth as shown.

Completed form.

what mix in the two egg yolks. Beat until stiff and then mix the beaten egg whites in a little at a time. Put the mixture in a small square pan and chill. When firm cut into 8 square blocks with a knife and serve 2 blocks per person.

Milk Jelly and Mixed Fruit

This jelly is made with isinglass. You should serve it with canned fruit. It makes an ideal light dessert one which is sure to please your family or friends.

INGREDIENTS (200 cal.)

- 1½ stick Japanese isinglass
- 2 tbs. sugar
- 2¼ cups milk
- small amt. essence of lemon
- 1 lb. can mixed fruit
- 3 tbs. sugar
- ½ cup water

PREPARATION

Break the isinglass up and soak it in water for about 30 minutes. Warm ⅓ of the milk. Squeeze the water out of the isinglass and put it in this milk. Stir while heating over a low flame until the isinglass dissolves. Add the sugar and when the milk boils turn the flame off. Pour the rest of the milk in. Add a little of essence of lemon for fragrance. Pour the liquid into a fairly large glass bowl and chill to harden.

Drain the liquid from the canned fruit and make a syrup out of it with the sugar and water. Cut the milk jelly into 1 in. squares in the bowl and carefully pour the syrup over it. The jelly will come floating up. Put the fruit on top of the jelly and serve.

Steamed Castile Cake

Castile cake from the region of the same name in Spain was introduced to Japan several centuries ago by traders who came to Nagasaki in Kyushu. This version is cooked in a steamer and should be eaten while still hot.

INGREDIENTS (270 cal.)

- 3½ oz. flour
- small amt. salt
- ½ tsp. baking powder
- 3 eggs

- 2¾ oz. sugar
- 2 tbs. fruit juice (from canned fruit)
- 1 can cherries or apricots
- 1 tbs. sugar
- 1 tbs. cornstarch
- 1 tbs. mirin or brandy

PREPARATION

Mix the flour, salt and the baking powder. Warm a bowl in lukewarm water and mix until the volume increases by three times. Thin the fruit juice (from canned fruit) with water and add it gradually to the mixed flour and baking powder. In the bottom of a small square wooden box or metal pan spread wax paper and pour the ingredients into it. Put the box in a steamer from which steam is issuing and steam for 15 minutes.

Separate the canned fruit from the juice; add the sugar to the juice and warm it. Make a paste from the cornstarch and water and mix with the juice. Add the mirin or brandy for fragrance.

Cut the steamed cake into sections and put the fruit on top. Pour the cornstarch fruit juice sauce over the top. Serve while still warm.

Tofu Dishes and Soups

Tofu and Mushroom Miso Soup, Tofu and Vegetables, Sweet-and-sour Meat Sauce, Deep Fried Tofu, Boiled Tofu, Fried Tofu, Fried Tofu in Miso Soup, "Harvest Moon" Chicken Soup, Lobster Soup

Tofu and Mushroom Miso Soup

Miso soup is the most common kind of soup in Japan. All families eat it and there are several hundred ways to make it. Dried bonito flakes and kelp are commonly used for the stock but artificial flavoring will do if you do not have these ingredients.

INGREDIENTS (33 cal.)

⅓ block tofu
5 mushrooms
3 cups chicken soup (should have no flavor to it)
2½ tbs. miso

PREPARATION

Cut the tofu into ½ inch blocks. Remove the mushroom stems and cut the tops into thin flakes. Mix the miso into the chicken soup and then the mushroom flakes and tofu blocks. Heat until boiling, then skim the surface and pour into soup bowls. If you have any sesame seeds heat some briefly in a pan; pound them lightly with a butcher knife and sprinkle on the soup. The fragrance is quite delightful.

Tofu and Vegetables

The tofu is crushed and mixed with vegetables, then heated again to harden it. A dish with a very simple taste.

INGREDIENTS (152 cal.)

2 blocks tofu
1 egg
2 tbs. sugar
½ tsp. salt
2 tsp. sake
1 tbs. shoyu
1 tbs. cornstarch

1 small carrot
5 mushrooms

10 string beans or 2 tbs. green peas
1 tbs. salad oil
1 tsp. sugar
¼ tsp. salt

PREPARATION

Heat water in a pan and put the tofu in as is to boil for 2 minutes. Remove the tofu from the pan, wrap in a cloth and firmly squeeze the water out. Put the tofu into a bowl and beat with a beater. While beating add the egg a little at a time. When mixed add the sugar, salt, sake, shoyu, and the cornstarch. Cut the carrot into long narrow strips and the mushrooms into thin slices.

Heat a tablespoon of salad oil in a frying pan and fry the carrot, mushrooms, and the string beans or green peas in that order. Then sprinkle the sugar and the salt on and turn off the flame. Mix this in with the beaten tofu and egg.

Put cooking oil on the bottom of a small square pan and line it with foil so that it can be easily removed later. Then pour your mixture into the pan. Steam this in a steamer on a medium flame for about 15 minutes. An alternative method is to fill a large shallow pan half full of boiling water and heat in an oven on medium heat so that the bottom does not burn. If, after you stick a toothpick in, clear liquid comes out turn off the heat. Cut into square bite-size pieces and serve. Can be eaten either hot or cold.

Sweet-and-sour Meat Sauce

This dish features a sweet and sour sauce of ground meat over tofu. It should be eaten while hot in order to enjoy the full flavor.

INGREDIENTS (180 cal.)

  2 blocks tofu
  7 oz. ground meat
  1 tsp. minced ginger root
  1 tbs. salad oil
  2½ tbs. shoyu
  1½ tbs. sugar
  1 tbs. sake
  ⅓ cup water
  artificial seasoning
  1 tbs. cornstarch
  1 leek

PREPARATION

Cut each tofu block into 6 pieces and put into rapidly boiling water. When the water begins to boil rapidly again turn the flame down low and let boil for 2 minutes. Pour the tofu out of the pan into a strainer so the water drains away.

Heat the salad oil and fry the ground meat and ginger in it. When it is well fried add the shoyu, sugar, sake, water, and the artificial seasoning and fry for two more minutes. Make a thick paste with the cornstarch and pour it into the pan. When the mixture takes on a mushy texture turn off the flame.

Cut the leek into small pieces and rinse with water. Then wrap it in a cloth and squeeze firmly to remove the water.

Take the thoroughly drained tofu and put 3 pieces in each person's plate. Pour meat sauce over the top and sprinkle the leek pieces on top of the sauce.

Deep Fried Tofu

This dish does not have a very long history-dating back only about 100 years. However, it is now a very popular dish. Tofu contains a great deal of vegetable protein and is excellent for weight-watchers.

INGREDIENTS (105 cal.)

  2 blocks tofu
  2 eggs
  small amt. flour
  small amt. oil
  ½ cup shoyu
  2 tbs. water
  4 tsp. grated ginger root

PREPARATION

Wrap the tofu in a cloth and gently press the water out. Cut each block into 8 pieces. Dust each piece with flour and pass it thru the well beaten eggs. Now dust each piece with flour once more.

Heat some oil to 360 degrees F. and deep fry the tofu being careful that it does not burn. (Tofu will not cause splattering of the oil even if there is moisture in it.)

Mix the shoyu and water and pour it over the fried tofu after placing the tofu on plates. Garnish with a little grated ginger and eat while still hot.

Deep fried tofu is delicious even with mayonnaise.

Boiled Tofu

This is a very common, economical, popular, and nourishing dish. Also it is easy to make and can be served year-round. During hot seasons you should cool the tofu in cold water after boiling it and then eat it with the sauce.

INGREDIENTS (130 cal.)

  3 blocks tofu
  1 cup shoyu
  8 in. length dried kelp (not essential)
  5 tbs. chopped leek
  1 tsp. grated ginger root
  small amt. shoyu

PREPARATION

Cut the tofu into 1¼ in. chunks. If you have the dried kelp wipe it with a wet cloth. Fill a pan 70% full of water and heat it. Add the kelp. When the water boils put the tofu in a little at a time. When the chunks come floating up they are done. Dip them out with a slotted spoon and they can be eaten immediately after dipping each bite into a sauce made from the grated ginger and the shoyu. The leftover kelp and water is not eaten as the kelp is simply for seasoning. If you have no dried kelp use artificial seasoning instead.

Fried Tofu

This dish was introduced into Japan from China about 700 years ago. At that time the tofu was fried in oil and eaten with a paste made of shoyu, cornstarch and Japanese horse-radish. The way we prepare it now is certain to please most anyone.

INGREDIENTS (314 cal.)

2 blocks tofu
1¼ in. carrot
5 mushrooms
12½ oz. chicken meat
5 tbs. shoyu
6½ tbs. sugar
3 tbs. water
3 eggs
1 tbs. sake (not essential)

PREPARATION

Wrap the tofu in a cloth and put something fairly heavy on top in order to press the water out. Leave this way for about one hour. Chop the carrot and mushrooms into fine pieces and cut the chicken meat into ½ in. chunks. Put all of this in a pot and add the shoyu, sugar, and the water. Boil until the liquid evaporates.

Break the tofu into little pieces with your hands and put them in the pot after mixing with the 3 eggs. If you have sake you can add it also. Heat another pot over a strong flame and when it is hot add the above ingredients to this pot stirring quickly and constantly so they will not burn. If you are not accustomed to doing this you might use a beater. When the eggs are all mixed in and there is almost no liquid left the dish is finished.

Fried Tofu in Miso Soup

For this dish we fry the tofu and then continue to use the same pan, tofu and all, to boil the soup. This is a simple dish—one which should go well at lunchtime.

INGREDIENTS (116 cal.)

⅓ block tofu
3 tbs. oil
3 cups water
2½ tbs. miso
small amt. finely chopped leeks or parsley

PREPARATION

Cut the tofu into ½ inch pieces. Heat some oil in a deep frying pan and fry the tofu without burning it or breaking it up. Now add the water and when the water boils put the miso in and dissolve it. Add the chopped leeks. (If you don't care for the smell of leeks used parsley instead.) When the liquid boils skim the surface before pouring the soup into bowls for serving.

"Harvest Moon" Chicken Soup

This soup takes its name from the egg yolk floating in the center of the soup bowl. We never use the egg white in clear soups such as this one.

INGREDIENTS (95 cal.)

3½ oz. chicken
¼ onion
4 egg yolks
3 cups water
1 tsp. salt
small amt. shoyu

PREPARATION

Cut the onion into thin slices and the chicken into ½ in. pieces. Heat the 3 cups of water in a pan and put the onion, chicken, salt, and the shoyu in and bring to a boil.

Put an egg yolk in each bowl without breaking the yolk. Pour the hot soup in each bowl and serve.

Lobster Soup

We have two main kinds of soup in Japan. The basic ingredient of the most common kind is simply fermented soybean paste (miso). This kind is sometimes made thicker with cornstarch or flour. This lobster soup which we give here is eaten only on special occasions in Japan.

INGREDIENTS (145 cal.)

2 lobster heads
1 block tofu
1½ tsp. salt
1 tsp. shoyu
5 cups water
1 leek sliced diagonally very thinly

PREPARATION

Chop the lobster heads in two.

Heat the 5 cups of water and when it boils put the lobster heads in. When the water boils once more skim the surface and then add the salt and shoyu for seasoning.

Cut the tofu into cubes about ¾ in. square and put them in the pot. Turn the heat off just before the liquid begins to boil again.

After dishing the soup into bowls sprinkle the leek slices onto the surface. (The soup will be even better if you leave the brain matter in the lobster heads.)

Fish Dishes

Salmon Steak, Country-style Boiled Abalone, Sweet-and-sour Boiled Scallops, Fish Teriyaki, and Cucumbers with Vinegared Miso, Prawns and Brussels Sprouts with Vinegared Shoyu, Lobster à la Egg Yolk Sauce, Grated Broccoli, Cold Fish Dish, Crab and Spinach with Mayonnaise-miso

Salmon Steak

A salmon steak with a delicious shoyu taste. Rainbow trout can also be used.

INGREDIENTS (154 cal)
 4 slices fresh salmon
 3 tbs. shoyu
 1½ tbs. mirin (Sake can be substituted. If you do, add 1 tsp. sugar.)
 1 piece ginger root
 2 leek
 3 tbs. flour
 2 tbs. salad oil
 1 tbs. butter
 1 head lettuce for salad
 2 tomatoes
 4 lemon slices

PREPARATION

Mix the shoyu and mirin (or sake and sugar). Grate the ginger and add it in together with the finely chopped leek. Drain the salmon and put it in this mixture for about 30 to 40 minutes.

Next drain the fish and cover very lightly with the flour. Heat the salad oil and butter in a frying pan and fry the fish on a medium flame until both sides take on a golden color.

Serve while hot with lemon slices on top and surrounded by chopped lettuce and tomato slices.

If the fish requires more flavor the sauce can be heated and poured over the fish according to individual taste.

Country-style Boiled Abalone

If a Japanese dish has "country-style" as a part of its name then you can be assured miso is used in preparing it. Actually miso is suitable for any kind of cooking. There are several kinds of miso; some light colored and others darker. The darker kind is best for this recipe. (A word of caution: This dish requires 7 to 8 hours of cooking.)

INGREDIENTS (140 cal.)
 14 oz. abalone
 20 mushrooms
 5 tbs. sake (or white wine)
 2 tbs. miso
 2 tbs. shoyu

PREPARATION

Whether the abalone is fresh or frozen rub salt into it and then wash well. Put in a pan with water so that it barely covers the abalone. Add the sake (or wine) and boil. Add water as needed and boil over a medium flame for 7 or 8 hours. When the abalone becomes soft add the miso, shoyu, and the mushrooms and boil further until the liquid has evaporated quite a bit.

Remove the abalone and mushrooms; cut into thin slices and serve.

Sweet-and-sour Boiled Scallops

This is a rather new dish to Japanese cooking but a popular one. If you and your family enjoy scallops you might like to try fixing them this way. Be careful not to over-boil either the scallops or the Brussels sprouts.

INGREDIENTS (134 cal.)
 24 small scallops or 4 large ones
 7 oz. Brussels sprouts
 4 tbs. shoyu
 5½ tbs. sugar
 5 tbs. water
 1 tbs. minced ginger root

PREPARATION

If you have the large scallops slice them into 2 or 3 thin slices each. If you have the small ones just wash them in salt water. Score the base of the Brussels sprouts and *quickly* boil them in water to which a little salt has been added. Drain well.

Put the water, shoyu, and the sugar in a pan and bring to a boil. When the liquid has boiled a few minutes add the Brussels sprouts and the scallops. Stir constantly and gently. Boil for only about 3 minutes then remove the entire contents and put on plates. Garnish with the minced ginger.

NOTE: If scallops are boiled too long they become hard and Brussels sprouts get too soft. If you're not careful, both will turn out poorly so boil the sauce before adding the scallops and sprouts. Then boil quickly over a strong flame being careful not to boil too long.

Sweet-and-sour Boiled Scallops

Fish Teriyaki

This is one of the simplest teriyaki recipes. In Japan we put the meat on skewers and cook it but even if you don't do it this way the taste will still be just as good. In place of fish, beef can also be used if you wish.

INGREDIENTS (315 cal.)
- 1½ lbs. fish (salmon, trout or any white meat fish)
- 1 tbs. sugar
- 4 tbs. shoyu
- 1 tbs. water
- artificial seasoning
- small amt. cooking oil
- small amt. grated giant white radish
- small amt. shoyu
- some cabbage or lettuce leaves

PREPARATION

Using the sections which have no bones cut the fish into servings of about 7 oz. each. Mix the sugar, shoyu, water, and the artificial seasoning and let the fish sit in this for about 10 minutes. (If you have some sake and mirin make this marinade sauce like this: To 2 parts sake and 3 parts mirin mix 4 parts shoyu. This makes a really tasty marinade and we recommend this one if you have the ingredients.)

Heat a frying pan and put the oil in it. Fry both sides of the fish and then pour the marinade in with the fish and continue frying until the liquid evaporates. Make a bed of cabbage or lettuce leaves on the plates and put the fish on top. Put the grated radish in a little mound on the front edge of each plate. (Squeeze the excess water out of the grated radish with your fingers.) Put a little shoyu on this grated radish mound and eat it together with the fish for added flavor.

Cuttlefish and Cucumbers with Vinegared Miso

Cucumbers in Japan are rather small as you can see if you look at the picture of them on the lobster. However, no matter what size cucumbers you have if they can be pickled then you can use them in this recipe.

INGREDIENTS (68 cal.)
- 1 medium size fresh cuttlefish
- 2 small cucumbers
- 5 tbs. miso
- 4 tbs. sugar
- 2 tbs. water
- 2 tbs. vinegar
- small amt. mustard
- small amt. salt

PREPARATION

With the exception of the legs, skin the cuttlefish and boil for only 10 to 20 seconds. Then quickly cool it under cold running water and cut into small strips of about 1¼ in. long.

Rub the salt into the cucumbers and then wash thoroughly. Cut them into the same size slices as you did the cuttlefish.

Mix the sugar with the miso. (According to the type of miso it might be necessary to add more or use less sugar. The taste is better when a little on the sweet side.) Add the water, make a paste of the miso and heat. Just before boiling add the vinegar. The resulting paste will be rather thick. Mix the mustard paste into this vinegared miso.

Put the cuttlefish and cucumber slices on a plate and cover with the vinegared miso just before eating.

Cuttlefish and Cucumbers with Vinegared Miso

Prawns and Brussels Sprouts with Vinegared Shoyu

Vinegar is used quite often in Japanese cooking and both prawns and Brussels sprouts go very well with it. Any prawns will do but remember not to boil them too long.

INGREDIENTS (136 cal.)
    4 prawns
    10½ oz. Brussels sprouts
    small amt. salt
    small amt. shoyu
    vinegared shoyu (4 tbs. vinegar and 1 tbs. shoyu mixed)

PREPARATION
Separate the prawn's heads from their tails and boil them in water with a little salt.

Remove the shells next and cut the meat in two the long way. (If you insert a sharp stick in along the prawn's back it will boil without twisting.)

With a knife score the base of the Brussels sprouts so they will cook thoroughly. Boil some water to which a little salt has been added. Put the sprouts in but not too long or they will lose their color. After boiling sprinkle a little shoyu into the scored area for seasoning.

Arrange the prawns and Brussels sprouts on plates and pour the vinegared shoyu sauce over just before eating.

Lobster à la Egg Yolk Sauce

The lobsters used in Japanese cooking are about 8 inches long and we usually serve one per person. However, if your lobsters are larger this will not be necessary.

INGREDIENTS (286 cal.)
    4 lobsters (assuming 4 persons will be eating and lobster size as explained above)
    2 cucumbers
    3 egg yolks
    3 tbs. water
    3 tbs. vinegar
    1 tsp. salad oil
    some leaves of lettuce or cabbage for salad

Prawns and Brussels sprouts with Vinegared Shoyu

PREPARATION

Boil the lobsters in water with a little salt. Remove the heads and take out the meat. Cut this meat into approximately ¼ in. thicknesses and pour a little shoyu over each piece.

Cut the hard parts of the skin off of the cucumbers and slice them into ⅛ in. pieces.

Put the egg yolks into a small pan and mix with the water and vinegar. Heat over a low flame while stirring and just before removing from heat add 1 tablespoon of salad oil. This will give you a rather thick vinegar egg yolk sauce.

Arrange the lobster and cucumber slices in the lobster shell on plates together with the lettuce or cabbage leaves. Pour the sauce on just before serving.

Grated Broccoli

Broccoli has been grown in Japan only a relatively short while and we even use the English name for it. Probably many Japanese have never had the experience of eating it but we thought you might enjoy fixing it this different way.

INGREDIENTS (52 cal.)

10½ oz. broccoli
7 oz. giant white Japanese radish
1 tbs. salmon roe
small amt. shoyu
2 tsp. vinegar
½ tsp. sugar
⅙ tsp. salt
½ lemon

PREPARATION

Break the broccoli down into bite-size chunks. Boil these chunks in some water to which a little salt has been added. Next put the broccoli on a plate and sprinkle a little shoyu over it.

Peel the white radish and grate it. Wring the excess moisture content out by squeezing it in your hands. Mix the gratings with the vinegar, sugar, salt, and the salmon roe. This is your sauce. Put the broccoli on a plate and just before eating pour this sauce over it. If you top it off with a little lemon squeezed over it the broccoli will improve even more in taste.

Cold Fish Dish

A Japanese-style dressing is put on fried fish while still hot. Then after the fish has cooled and the flavor has developed it is served.

INGREDIENTS (166 cal.)

14 oz. white fish meat (mackerel, sardine, etc.)
small amt. salt
3 tbs. cornstarch
cooking oil
3 tbs. vinegar
2 tbs. water
2 tbs. sugar
2 tbs. shoyu
⅓ tsp. salt
1 red pepper
1 piece ginger root
3 green onions
2 cucumbers
small amt. salt

PREPARATION

Remove the fish bones and cut the fish lengthwise so it will be easy to eat. Sprinkle salt on and let sit for five minutes.

Mix the vinegar, sugar, shoyu, and the salt. Remove the red pepper seeds and cut it length-wise so each piece is a small circle. Cut up the ginger very thinly and cut the green onions in fine slices starting from the edge. Mix all of this together and spread onto a platter.

Heat the cooking oil in a pan. Dust the fish in the cornstarch and after shaking off the excess put each piece in the pan. Fry it

Grated Broccoli

quickly on a medium flame for about 2 to 3 minutes. Take out and drain the oil off. Then while still hot put the fish on the platter and turn it so that the mixture thoroughly covers the fish. Then leave to sit for about 30 minutes.

Cut the cucumber in thin circle slices, sprinkle a little salt on and let sit for a few minutes. When the moisture starts to come out squeeze the cucumber firmly and then serve alongside each piece of fish.

Crab and Spinach with Mayonnaise-miso

In Japan we eat spinach quite a bit and in a number of different ways. We use spinach in soups and pickled and sometimes just boiled as in this dish.

INGREDIENTS (196 cal.)
    1 can of canned crab (approx. 6½ oz.)
    10½ oz. spinach
    small amt. shoyu
    6 tbs. mayonnaise
    1 tbs. miso
    small amt. shoyu
PREPARATION
Take the crab meat out of the can and remove any bones. Boil the spinach quickly so it keeps its color in some water to which a little salt has been added. Squeeze the water out of the spinach (wrap it in a cloth for this

purpose) and pour on a little shoyu for flavoring. Now squeeze the spinach once again and cut it into about 1¼ in. length.

Mix the mayonnaise and miso and add a little shoyu to season.

Put the crab and spinach on a plate and add the mayonnaise-miso. If you want to add a Japanese touch take a cucumber and cut it as shown in the illustration. Then fold the slices down as shown and you have a "folding fan" to add interest to the dish. (see illustration)

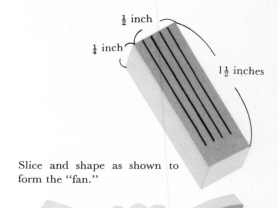

Slice and shape as shown to form the "fan."

Lobster à la Egg Yolk Sauce

Crab and Spinach with Mayonnaise-miso